Sherryism's

Sherry Anshara

Design: Amit Dey
Published by: Spotlight Publishing™
https://spotlightpublishing.pro

Website: www.sherryanshara.com

Sherryism's

Introduction

"Make each moment count...
because each moment belongs to you!"

~ Sherryism

The focus of this Sherryism Book is for you, the reader,
to "listen", "observe" and perhaps view life through
more expanded lenses of language and words.

What is underlying the "face value" of statements? Let
these Sherryisms support you to vision your life through
your expansion of your vision of life and what life can
mean for you...

Full of Meaning!

Enjoy!

Your heart is the most expansion
resonance in your body.
When judgment is in your heart,
all you heart can do is resonant
judgment of Self and others.

Put your heart into something you love,
not into something
that shuts your heart down.

Your Heart is smarter than
your left computer/brain...
Listen to your smart heart!"

When your heart is blocked,
your life is blocked.

So if you are born to die,
then why show up?
You are born to live!

Could it be that where you go after you die,
is the place you believe you are going!

Life is meant to live and be lively!

Instead of a good day to die,
how about this is a good day to live!

Stop running and step forward into life,
it is so much easier!

Think too much... you stop your creativity!

Life may not be what you "think"
it is...
Life is what you create when
you stop thinky thinking about it!

How you invest your time,
is how time pays off.
Invest wisely in how you spend your time!

"Changes come from the inside when you let go of the outside!"

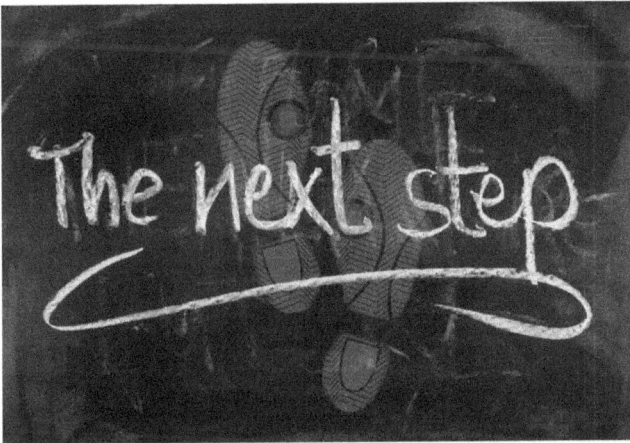

Not ready?
Are you stuck in the avoidance of denial?
Are you living on the Nile river in Egypt...
in your past?

How do you know the grass is always greener on the other side of the fence since you are the one who put up the fence?

If your now is based on then,
and your then was a mess, let it go.
Leave it in the past,
and create a "New Now."
It is how you choose the New Now that counts!

The fairy tale nightmare?
Grow up, get married, have children,
and live happily ever after.
After What?
No one asked what?

Start asking Your Self...
What is my life all about for me?

If your Princess or Prince
turns into a Bitch...
B-itch means being the itch.
What's bugging you,
that you are blaming on her or him?
Often it turns out to be...
it is truly all about you.
What's the Self-itch that is irritating you?

The only way out of an issue
is the way inside your Self
to find where the issue is stuck!

Believe in Your Self
and life believes in you!

Not to believe in your Self
is a Duality B.S. Program!

What separates humans from humans,
from each other,
is the limiting
Duality Belief Systems of separation!

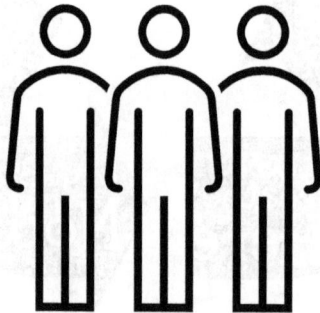

Believe in Your Self
and
your Life is Believable!

Listen to your body.
Stop hearing your left
Duality computer brain!

JUST
BE

Your body is your intelligence,
your brain only computes limitations.
STOP THINKY-THINKING!

Your conscious mind,
not your Duality computer/brain,
is a wonderful place to expand!

When your computer/brain is up yours,
then it is challenged to know
the difference between the
B.S and the TRUTH!

Centered in Self
is much more productive than being
Self-Centered!

ISIN
IS IN
or I SIN

hmmmmmm!

What's the point?
If something doesn't make sense,
then what sense is the point!

Stories belong in fairy tales.
Create experiences.
Forget the fairy tales.
Live Consciously!

If your prince charming
turns into a frog...
stop croaking,
and move on!

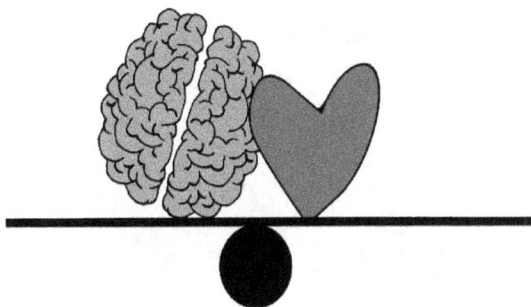

Wanty-needy relationships...
you can't save anyone.
So, stop being a life-raft,
throw out a life saver,
and share the pack!

"Programs for Sale or Rent,"
The "wanty-needy" country song
"I can't live without you,"
So...!

Birds of feather may flock together.
Sometimes it is time to leave the nest,
and explore on your own!

"EST" in Latin
means "To Be"...
"To Be" is up to you...
Be Great
Why not?

Computer brain logic is the
LOG-I-"C" that blocks my way.
So much for logic!
Be open, it is so much easier to thrive!

Stay out of your computer/brain head.
Let your heart lead your way!

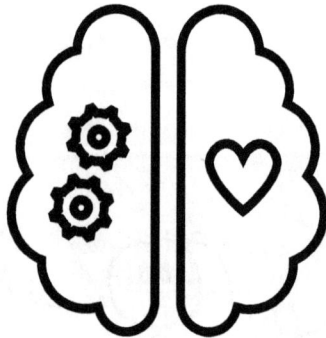

"Your heart knows the Truth.
Your head knows the Duality True
Programs.
It is your choice!"

Dogma spelled backward spells
AM GOD
Hmmmm!

"Con"trol
Hmmmm...
In Wordology is Your Biology,
isn't it the "con"
of the little unconscious "troll"
inside you, who makes your life miserable?

Hmmmm!

Food for thought
Are you craving changes,
but still eating the same old indigestible
Duality B.S.?"

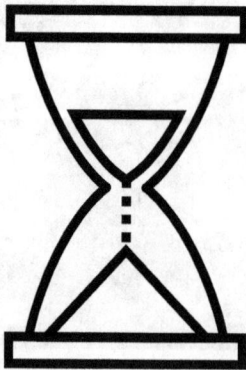

The Question is not...
"Is your glass half empty or half full?"
Find out what it is full of,
and if you don't like it,
take the empty glass,
and fill it full of your life!

Stop running and step forward
into your life,
it is so much easier!

What counts, is
not how fast you go.
It is how you go through life
that counts!

Go along for the ride as long as you can
"see" where the ride is taking you!

How you spend your time depends upon the
costs you are willing to spend or not!

If life is in the palms of your hands,
stop making fists...
you block your life!

Think as though you have a block.
Block means you are B-eing the Lock.
You are the key to unlocking the block!

The best part of life is the part of life in which you take part in your best part!

Trying and trying and trying is so trying.
So, stop trying.

Do it or not!

Baggage is what you bagged
at a particular age.
Luggage is the baggage you drag around...
Time to let go and move forward!

Read the "con"tract
before you contract
someone into your life!

Love is blind.
Perhaps the hormones
are blocking your eyesight!

Caller ID was invented
to give you time to prepare
for whomever is on the
other end of the phone!

With each ending
is a new beginning,
a fabulous cycle of life!

When something is meaningful,
make sure it is not full of mean,
but full of meaning!

Time is best used
when you don't let time use you up!

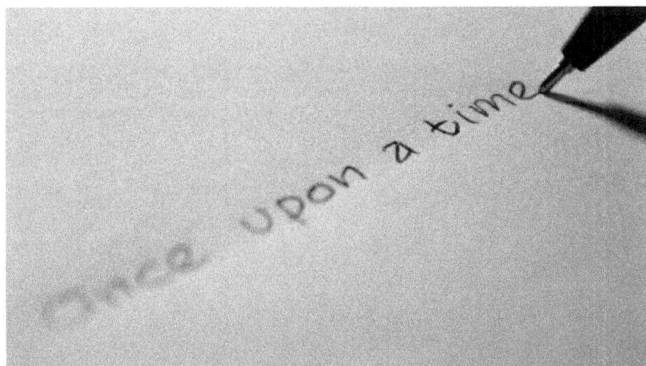

If you have a Belief System, (B.S.)
that karma is real,
then death is not an end result.
It is a do-over Duality program...
Oops... "I did it again!"